CELEBRATING OUR HOLIDAYS

I0801050

Celebrating THANKSGIVING

BY ELIZABETH MORGAN AND
ELAINE LANDAU

Cavendish Square
New York

Published in 2023 by Cavendish Square Publishing, LLC
29 E. 21st Street New York, NY 10010

Copyright © 2023 by Cavendish Square Publishing, LLC

No part of this publication may be reproduced, stored in a retrieval system, or transmitted in any form or by any means—electronic, mechanical, photocopying, recording, or otherwise—without the prior permission of the copyright owner. Request for permission should be addressed to Permissions, Cavendish Square Publishing, 29 E. 21st Street New York, NY 10010. Tel (877) 980-4450; fax (877) 980-4454.

Website: cavendishsq.com

This publication represents the opinions and views of the author based on their personal experience, knowledge, and research. The information in this book serves as a general guide only. The author and publisher have used their best efforts in preparing this book and disclaim liability rising directly or indirectly from the use and application of this book.

Disclaimer: Portions of this work were originally authored by Elaine Landau and published as *Thanksgiving Day: A Time to Be Thankful.* All new material in this edition authored by Elizabeth Morgan.

All websites were available and accurate when this book was sent to press.

Library of Congress Cataloging-in-Publication Data

Names: Morgan, Elizabeth, 1993- author. | Landau, Elaine, author.
Title: Celebrating thanksgiving / Elizabeth Morgan, Elaine Landau.
Description: New York : Cavendish Square Publishing, 2023. | Series: Celebrating our holidays | Includes index.
Identifiers: LCCN 2021041835 | ISBN 9781502664853 (set) | ISBN 9781502664860 (library binding) | ISBN 9781502664846 (paperback) | ISBN 9781502664877 (ebook)
Subjects: LCSH: Thanksgiving Day–Juvenile literature.
Classification: LCC GT4975 .M68 2023 | DDC 394.2649–dc23
LC record available at https://lccn.loc.gov/2021041835

Editor: Katie Kawa
Copyeditor: Jill Keppeler
Designer: Deanna Paternostro

The photographs in this book are used by permission and through the courtesy of: Cover, p. 1 Bochkarev Photography/Shutterstock.com; back cover, pp. 3, 5, 6, 9, 13, 15, 19, 21, 23, 25, 27, 28, 29, 30, 31, 32 N.D.Vector/Shutterstock.com; p. 4 Monkey Business Images/Shutterstock.com; pp. 7, 23 Brent Hofacker/Shutterstock.com; pp. 8, 12, 17 Everett Collection/Shutterstock.com; p. 11 Morphart Creation/Shutterstock.com; p. 14 LightField Studios/Shutterstock.com; p. 18 Simfalex/Shutterstock.com; p. 20 Hurst Photo/Shutterstock.com; p. 22 Peiling Lee/Shutterstock.com; p. 24 TD Dolci/Shutterstock.com; p. 26 WoodysPhotos/Shutterstock.com; p. 27 BAZA Production/Shutterstock.com; p. 28 deannalindsey/Shutterstock.com.

Some of the images in this book illustrate individuals who are models. The depictions do not imply actual situations or events.

CPSIA compliance information: Batch #CSCSQ23: For further information contact Cavendish Square Publishing LLC, New York, New York, at 1-877-980-4450.

Printed in the United States of America

Find us on

CONTENTS

All across the United States, families gather together on Thanksgiving to share a meal and enjoy each other's company. Some people travel a long way to be with their family on this holiday!

CHAPTER ONE

A Day to Give Thanks

What are you thankful for? That question is asked a lot on Thanksgiving—a day set aside for thinking about the things in our lives we're grateful for. Many people are thankful for their family and friends, and they share a meal with them on this day. Thanksgiving dinner is a popular **tradition** throughout the United States, and the roots of this holiday reach back to the time before the country was founded.

The history of Thanksgiving is connected to the history of colonization—the process by which Europeans came to lands indigenous, or native, peoples lived on and took control of them. The stories we know about U.S. history, including the history of Thanksgiving, are often one-sided, leaving out how Native Americans really felt or thought about events. Today, though, many people are working to find out the whole story, including the Native American point of view.

A Harvest Holiday

Thanksgiving is held on the fourth Thursday of November every year in the United States. This time of year is often **associated** with harvesting—when seeds that were planted become crops that can be collected and eaten. In fact, what we think of as the first Thanksgiving, which took place in the 1600s, was a harvest celebration. Some of the people who gathered together for it were thankful for a successful harvest.

Many Thanksgiving decorations, stories, and more focus on the Pilgrims and a group of Native Americans. They were present at what's now known as the first Thanksgiving celebration. The Pilgrims came to what's now the United States from England in 1620, while many Native American groups had lived on this land for many years before the Pilgrims arrived. The situation was much more complicated than simply having a party, but the groups did come together, likely to celebrate the harvest. Many people remember that celebration today when they eat their own Thanksgiving meals.

Food and Fun

Food plays a big part in many families' Thanksgiving celebrations. Some people spend many hours preparing their Thanksgiving dinner. Families often cook together or bring dishes to share with one another.

Different Days to Give Thanks

Not every country celebrates Thanksgiving. In addition, many countries that celebrate a similar holiday do so on a different date than the United States. For example, Thanksgiving is also a popular holiday in Canada. However, it's held in October rather than November. Other countries that have their own **versions** of Thanksgiving include Germany, Japan, and the Netherlands, which was where some of the Pilgrims lived before coming to what's now the United States.

Many people have their own special recipes for Thanksgiving foods.

Popular Thanksgiving foods include turkey, cranberry sauce, and pumpkin pie. These fall foods honor the harvest roots of the holiday. However, many historians believe they weren't on the table at the harvest meal people now call the first Thanksgiving. That celebration looked very different from the Thanksgiving meals we share today.

The Pilgrims came to what's now the United States to find a place where they could make more money and practice their religion, or belief system, as they wanted to. They had religious freedom in the Netherlands, where they lived after leaving England at first, but many didn't like it there.

CHAPTER TWO

HOW IT BEGAN

The Thanksgiving celebrations we have today have roots that can be traced back more than 400 years. When the Pilgrims first came to what's now the United States, life wasn't easy. They struggled to **survive**, but that struggle may have helped them see what they had to be thankful for.

MAKING THE TRIP ON THE *MAYFLOWER*

In September 1620, the Pilgrims began their trip across the Atlantic Ocean on a ship called the *Mayflower*. There were storms at sea, and the passengers were often seasick. Finally, in November 1620, the Pilgrims spotted land in today's Massachusetts. This was where they would settle—nearby in a colony they called Plymouth.

Although the Pilgrims were happy to have reached land, their first months in America were even worse than their time at sea. They faced a very harsh winter, and they didn't have enough food. Many Pilgrims became ill, and some of them died. By spring, only about 50 of the 102 people who'd traveled on the *Mayflower* were alive.

The Pilgrims refused to give up, but things were still hard. They tried to plant crops from seeds they'd brought from England. However, the seeds wouldn't grow well. The Pilgrims also didn't know the land well enough to hunt or catch fish successfully. They needed help.

Native American Allies

Various Native American groups lived around the Pilgrims' settlement, but the Native Americans and Pilgrims didn't speak to one another for many months. That changed on March 16, 1621. On that day, a Native American man named Samoset greeted the Pilgrims by saying, "Welcome." The Pilgrims were very surprised to learn that Samoset spoke English. He'd learned the language from English fishermen who came to what's now Maine each year to fish.

Samoset knew the area around Plymouth well. A Native American village had once existed there, but it had been wiped out by sickness. Samoset later returned with another Native American, Tisquantum, who's better known by the name Squanto. Like Samoset, Squanto also spoke English. He learned it years before, when he was taken by the English and sold into slavery.

Squanto helped the Pilgrims as a guide and adviser. He stayed with them for several months and told them which crops to grow. Squanto gave the Pilgrims seeds for corn, squash, and pumpkins. Other vegetables were planted too. He taught them to bury a dead fish wherever they planted seeds. This made the soil healthier.

Squanto also took the Pilgrims into the forest. The men learned to hunt for deer, rabbits, and wild turkeys. In addition, Squanto taught them to make good use of the waters in the area. Before long, the Pilgrims were trapping lobsters and digging for clams.

The Native Americans who reached out to the Pilgrims did so as part of a plan to gain allies to help in their conflicts with other groups.

Time to Eat

Squanto helped the Pilgrims survive and establish a successful settlement. By fall 1621, the Pilgrims had a decent harvest. There was enough food for the coming winter. They decided to celebrate with a feast.

Native Americans from the Wampanoag people came to the feast too. They didn't come empty-handed. The 90 Wampanoag guests brought five deer, so there was plenty of food for everyone.

The foods they ate were not what many of us eat on Thanksgiving today. There was the venison (deer) that the Wampanoag brought, in addition to fish and shellfish. There were many wild turkeys around Plymouth, but it's not known if turkey was eaten at this celebration.

The first feast shared by the Pilgrims and the Wampanoag in fall 1621 was most likely very different from the ideas—and the art—we have about it today.

THE WAMPANOAG PEOPLE

The Native Americans who joined the Pilgrims at their harvest feast were members of the Wampanoag group. Squanto lived with a group of Wampanoag peoples known as the Pokanoket. Their leader was named Ousamequin but is often known as Massasoit—a term that means "Grand Sachem." A sachem is a leader of a certain Native American group. Ousamequin ruled over a period of peace with the Pilgrims, but it ended soon after his death.

No one knows the exact days when the celebration took place, but it was probably sometime in the fall—between September and November. The feast lasted three days and featured games and other activities.

The Pilgrims didn't think of this celebration as a time for giving thanks. For them, giving thanks to God meant hours of prayer and fasting instead of eating. This was simply a time to enjoy a good harvest before a long winter.

This feast wasn't held every year. Some years, crops failed, and there was little reason to celebrate. However, in 1623, a feast **specifically** meant for giving thanks was celebrated, but historians believe this feast may have taken place in the summer.

Over time, the idea of coming together over a big meal to give thanks began to catch on, and Thanksgiving as we celebrate it today began to take shape.

In the United States, Thanksgiving is a national holiday. This means that it's celebrated across the country. It wasn't always a national holiday, though.

CHAPTER THREE

Celebrations Spread

Although what we think of as the first Thanksgiving was celebrated more than 400 years ago, it took a long time for it to become the beloved national holiday it is today. Harvest celebrations such as the one the Pilgrims had weren't celebrated every year, and they weren't celebrated all across the British colonies that would become the United States. Many years had to pass and hard work had to happen to make Thanksgiving a national holiday.

Thanksgiving in the New Nation

Different Thanksgiving celebrations were held throughout the British colonies in America. During the American Revolution—when the colonists fought for freedom from British rule from 1775 to 1783—several days were set aside for giving thanks. These days were usually after important victories. The first Thanksgiving Day for the entire United States, however, was not until November 26, 1789. President George Washington ordered it, but it didn't become a national tradition yet.

In time, some states established their own Thanksgiving Day. New York was one of the first states to do so. By 1817, Thanksgiving was celebrated every year in New York. Other northern states did the same thing, and southern states joined in too. Each state celebrated Thanksgiving on a day of its choosing. There was no standard Thanksgiving Day like there is today.

Sarah Hale's Hard Work

By the middle of the 1800s, many states had their own Thanksgiving Day celebrations. There seemed to be little need to make this day a national holiday. However, Sarah Josepha Hale felt differently.

Hale was a magazine editor. Every fall, she filled her magazine with Thanksgiving stories, songs, and recipes. She wrote about how this day should be a national holiday because the United States didn't have enough holidays.

Hale then began writing letters to governors, members of Congress, and even presidents about her cause. In 1863, her hard work paid off when President Abraham Lincoln declared a national day of Thanksgiving for the whole country on the last Thursday of November. Hale's part in making this happen earned her the nickname "The Mother of Thanksgiving."

The Nation Celebrates

The tradition of declaring a national day of Thanksgiving on the last Thursday of November lasted for more than 70 years. Although it was still not a federal holiday—a holiday officially named by the U.S. government—it was celebrated by Americans across the country.

In 1939, President Franklin D. Roosevelt changed the holiday to the third Thursday of November. This was a week earlier than usual. The president wanted to help American businesses. He hoped making the holiday earlier would make the Christmas shopping season last longer. However, this idea didn't last long.

Abraham Lincoln was president during the American Civil War, which was fought from 1861 to 1865. This war saw the country split as a number of Southern states formed the Confederate States of America. Lincoln believed a day of giving thanks in the middle of the war would be good for the American people.

Franklin D. Roosevelt changed the date of Thanksgiving to help businesses during the Great Depression, which was a time when many Americans lost their jobs.

Federal Holidays

Thanksgiving is one of many federal holidays celebrated in the United States. The others are:

- New Year's Day (January 1)
- the birthday of Dr. Martin Luther King Jr. (third Monday of January)
- the birthday of George Washington, also known as Presidents' Day (third Monday of February)
- Memorial Day (last Monday of May)
- Juneteenth (June 19)
- Independence Day (July 4)
- Labor Day (first Monday of September)
- Columbus Day, also known as Indigenous Peoples' Day (second Monday of October)
- Veterans Day (November 11)
- Christmas Day (December 25)

Congress finally made things official in 1941, when Thanksgiving Day was declared a federal holiday. The date was changed to the fourth Thursday in November. On that day, all government offices are closed. In addition, schools, banks, and many businesses are closed as well. There's no mail delivery. In homes throughout the nation, people celebrate the day and give thanks. Some traditions differ from family to family, but many are shared by all Americans—beginning with what's for dinner.

Although every family celebrates Thanksgiving in their own way, some traditional foods are common sights on nearly every Thanksgiving dinner table.

CHAPTER FOUR

A HARVEST FEAST

Thanksgiving as Americans celebrate it today began as a harvest feast. Similar celebrations of a good harvest can be found throughout history—long before the Pilgrims came to Plymouth. These celebrations all featured lots of good food. That tradition of celebrating with food and family hasn't been lost over the centuries. In fact, food is the most famous part of Thanksgiving celebrations in the United States.

ANCIENT CELEBRATIONS

Food has always been a reason to celebrate for people around the world. Some of these celebrations date back to ancient times. The names and dates may be different, but the idea behind them is the same. When enough food is grown to keep people healthy and happy, it's time to celebrate!

Ancient Romans held a festival, or celebration, known as Cerelia (also spelled Cerealia or Ceríalia). They honored Ceres, the goddess of farming—especially the farming of grains. In fact, the name Ceres is where we get the word "cereal."

For thousands of years, Chinese people have celebrated the harvest season with a fall festival. It's known as the Moon Festival or the Mid-Autumn Festival. Harvest fruits, such as grapes, play

Every group has its own sweet treat to share at harvest celebrations. Americans have pumpkin pie, but Chinese people eat moon cakes such as the ones shown here.

a big part in the celebrations even today. In addition, small, round cakes known as moon cakes have been popular Moon Festival treats for many years.

Jewish people also have a festival of giving thanks called Sukkot (also spelled Sukkoth). Sukkot began thousands of years ago and is still celebrated every fall. Some families build a small hut for the festival. Leaves are spread over its roof. Apples, grapes, corn, and other vegetables are hung inside, and families eat dinner in the hut. This festival is celebrated by Jewish people around the world, including in the United States.

Thanksgiving Dinner

Harvest festivals around the world each have their own special foods, and Thanksgiving is no different. Most people eat turkey on Thanksgiving. In fact, about 45 million turkeys are eaten every year on this day. Sweet potatoes and mashed potatoes are often eaten too. Corn is another popular Thanksgiving food that can be traced all the way back to the Pilgrims. Many Americans also make stuffing for Thanksgiving, which involves mixing cubes of bread, celery, onions, and other ingredients together.

For dessert, pies are the sweet treat of choice for most Americans. Pumpkin pie is the most popular Thanksgiving dessert, and more than 50 million pumpkin pies are eaten every year on this holiday.

Some foods, such as cranberry sauce, are common parts of nearly every Thanksgiving dinner in the United States.

Not every dinner table looks the same on Thanksgiving, though. People from different **cultures** often make foods that are special to them in addition to traditional Thanksgiving dishes. For example, people whose families came to the United States from Italy often make pasta dishes to go along with their turkey and stuffing. It's fun to combine traditional Thanksgiving foods with your family's favorites.

Doing It Differently

No two families celebrate Thanksgiving the exact same way. Some people are vegetarian, or don't eat meat, so they don't have a Thanksgiving turkey. Native Americans have been sharing Thanksgiving recipes for foods that are more closely connected to their history, such as fry bread and desserts with wild berries. Some people make all their food themselves, while others buy some or all of it from a store or a restaurant. There isn't one right way to celebrate this holiday.

The Macy's Thanksgiving Day Parade is held every year in New York City. Many people watch it on TV as part of their Thanksgiving Day traditions.

CHAPTER FIVE

Other Ways We Celebrate

Food is the main focus of Thanksgiving for many people, but making and eating a big dinner isn't the only tradition families have on this holiday. Some families watch a parade together in the morning. Others watch a football game at night. Still others see Thanksgiving as a day to give back to their community. No matter how people choose to celebrate, Thanksgiving is often a day of fun, family, and feeling grateful.

A Popular Parade

Parades are a popular part of Thanksgiving in the United States, and one parade stands out above the rest: Macy's Thanksgiving Day Parade. It's known as the world's largest parade, and people from around the world visit New York City to see it in person every year. Millions more watch it on TV from their homes.

The parade has marching bands and clowns. There are also huge balloons filled with helium, a gas that's lighter than air. It allows the giant balloons to float high above the crowds. The balloons are shaped like well-known cartoon and movie characters, such as Olaf from the *Frozen* movies and Spider-Man. In addition, floats carry many famous singers down the parade route, and Santa Claus even makes an appearance!

A Day to Play

The Pilgrims and Native Americans are believed to have played games when they gathered for their harvest feast. Today, games and sports are still important parts of some Thanksgiving celebrations.

Many Americans watch football on Thanksgiving Day. The National Football League (NFL) holds three games on Thanksgiving that are shown around the country on TV. Two of those games feature the Detroit Lions and Dallas Cowboys each playing a different team every year.

Races are held around the country on Thanksgiving too. Many are known as "turkey trots." They often help raise money for groups that feed the hungry in the community where the race is held. Taking part in one of these races is a great way to have fun while helping others.

A Helping Hand

Thanksgiving is often seen as a day to think about what we're thankful for and to think about the ways we can help people who are less fortunate. One way to help is through Thanksgiving food drives. People can **donate** food to organizations that feed the hungry. Many

Some races, such as the one shown here, are held the day after Thanksgiving. This keeps the fun going all weekend!

schools hold their own Thanksgiving food drives. There are other, more hands-on, ways to help too.

Soup kitchens and homeless shelters feed the homeless and hungry all year, but they are especially busy on Thanksgiving. Many host special holiday dinners. Volunteers spend the day helping. They cook and serve the food and clean up afterward. Some families volunteer together.

Volunteering at a soup kitchen or homeless shelter with your family is a great way to help other people have a happy Thanksgiving too.

Helping others is a great way to remember all we have to be thankful for. That's the meaning of this special day. Football games, parades, and big dinners are fun, but they're not what Thanksgiving is all about. It's a day to be grateful for all we've been given and to share those feelings of thankfulness with family and friends.

A Presidential Pardon

Thanksgiving isn't much fun for turkeys. That's why before every Thanksgiving, the president of the United States **pardons** at least one very lucky turkey. This means the bird never reaches a dinner table. Instead, it goes to a farm to live the rest of its life there. This fun tradition officially began with President George H. W. Bush in 1989, although some presidents before him, such as Ronald Reagan and John F. Kennedy, unofficially pardoned Thanksgiving turkeys.

MAKE A PINE CONE TURKEY

YOU WILL NEED:

1 pine cone

7–10 cotton swabs (or more depending on the size of the pinecone)

markers or paints and paintbrush (colors: red, yellow, and orange)

orange felt

scissors

2 googly eyes

glue

This turkey will look cute on any Thanksgiving dinner table!

Directions:

1. Color the cotton swabs using markers or paint. Allow them to dry before the next step.
2. Glue the googly eyes to the front of the pine cone.
3. Cut a small triangle from the orange felt.
4. Glue the triangle under the eyes to make the turkey's nose.
5. **Attach** the cotton swabs around the pine cone to make the turkey's tail feathers. If they won't stick into the pine cone on their own, use glue to hold them in place.

GLOSSARY

associate: To think of one person or thing when you think of another person or thing.

attach: To join one thing to another.

culture: The beliefs and ways of life of a certain group of people.

donate: To give something in order to help a person or organization.

pardon: To officially say that someone does not have to pay a debt and can go free without being punished.

specifically: In a definite and exact way.

survive: To keep living.

tradition: A way of thinking, behaving, or doing something that's been used by people in a particular society for a long time.

version: A form of something that is different from others.

FIND OUT MORE

Books

Markovics, Pearl. *Thanksgiving*. Minneapolis, MN: Bearport Publishing, 2019.

Messner, Kate. *The Mayflower*. New York, NY: Random House, 2020.

Romero, Libby. *The Mayflower*. New York, NY: DK Publishing, 2020.

Websites

The First Thanksgiving
kids.nationalgeographic.com/history/article/first-thanksgiving
Visitors to this *National Geographic Kids* page will find plenty of fun facts about what we think of as the first Thanksgiving.

Plimoth Patuxet Museums
plimoth.org/
Visit this website to learn more about the history of Thanksgiving and to plan a trip to a place that brings Plymouth Colony to life for people today.

Publisher's note to educators and parents: Our editors have carefully reviewed these websites to ensure that they are suitable for students. Many websites change frequently, however, and we cannot guarantee that a site's future contents will continue to meet our high standards of quality and educational value. Be advised that students should be closely supervised whenever they access the Internet.

INDEX